The *Condottieri*: The History of Italy's Elite Mercenaries during the Middle Ages and Renaissance

By Charles River Editors

A contemporary fresco depicting some Italian soldiers

About Charles River Editors

Charles River Editors provides superior editing and original writing services across the digital publishing industry, with the expertise to create digital content for publishers across a vast range of subject matter. In addition to providing original digital content for third party publishers, we also republish civilization's greatest literary works, bringing them to new generations of readers via ebooks.

About the Author

Sean McLachlan is an historian and archaeologist who has explored ancient sites throughout Europe and the Middle East. He has written numerous books and articles on history and is also the author of several works of fiction, including the _Masked Man of Cairo_ series of historical mystery novels and the Civil War horror novel _A Fine Likeness_. Learn more about his work on his Amazon page and Facebook page.

Introduction

Portrait of a condottiero **by Ermanno Stroiffi**

"None of the principal states were armed with their own proper forces. Thus the arms of Italy were either in the hands of the lesser princes, or of men who possessed no state; for the minor princes did not adopt the practice of arms from any desire of glory, but for the acquisition of either property or safety. The others (those who possessed no state) being bred to arms from their infancy, were acquainted with no other art, and pursued war for emolument, or to confer honor upon themselves." – Machiavelli

In 1494, there were five sovereign regional powers in Italy: Milan, Venice, Florence, the Papal States and Naples. In 1536, only one remained: Venice. These decades of conflict precipitated great anxiety among Western thinkers, and Italians responded to the fragmentation, forevermore, of Latin Christendom, the end of self-governance for Italians, and the beginning of the early modern era in a myriad of ways. They were always heavily influenced by the lived experience of warfare between large Christian armies on the peninsula.

The diplomatic and military history of this 30 year period was a complex one that one eminent Renaissance historian, Lauro Martines, described as "best told by a computer, so many and tangled are the treatises, negotiations and battles."[1] The fighting went in tandem with the Renaissance and was influenced by it, and the Venetian involvement in the Holy League and the successful restoration of the Aragonese dynasty in Naples served as catalysts for the development of a political and ideological orientation that was shared by the ruling classes across the Italian peninsula. The catch phrases for this movement were *buoni italiani* and *libertà d'Italia*. These terms described the proponents of a strategic line that attempted to revive the political systems in force in Italy at a perceived time of "political balance" between the Peace of Lodi in 1454 and the French invasion of 1494.[2] As a political program, the *libertà d'Italia* demanded the expulsion of the transalpine foreigners from Italy and the reconstruction of a multi-state structure that was balanced and ruled by natives.[3] That would not truly occur until the 19th century, and Italy would serve as a theater of war for the Hapsburg and Valois monarchies until the mid-16th century, until the Peace of Cateau-Cambrésis in 1559.

Since several large city-states such as Milan and Venice growing rich on the prosperous Mediterranean trade routes, they had the money to commission grandiose cathedrals and works of art that still astound people today, but they also had the resources to hire armies and constantly fight to expand their power. Ironically, their very success was an impediment, as most prosperous city-states had far more money than available manpower because so many people worked in essential jobs in agriculture, crafts, or public works. Large bodies of men could not be spared for fighting, so if a city-state wanted to expand, it needed to hire an army to bolster the ranks.

Other factors limited the use of homegrown armies. City militias often got embroiled in the factional disputes that were rife in Italian urban politics, to the extent that the militia might take one side or another, or be so divided as to be ineffective against external enemies. The only way

---

[1] Lauro Martines, *Power and Imagination: City-States in Renaissance Italy* (Baltimore: Johns Hopkins Press, 1979), 277. The best overviews of the Italian Wars in English are Gene Brucker's 'A Horseshoe Nail': Structure and Contingency in Medieval and Renaissance Italy," in *Living on the Edge in Leonardo's Florence* (Berkeley, Los Angeles and London: University of California Press, 2005): 62-82 and Michael Mallet and Christine Shaw, *The Italian Wars, 1494-1559* (Harlow: Pearson, 2012). See also Jean-Louis Fournel and Jean-Claude Zancarini, *Les guerres d'Italie: Des batailles pour l'Europe (1494-1559)* (Paris: Gallimard, 2003), and Marco Pellegrini, *Le guerre d'Italia (1494-1530)* (Bologna: Il Mulino, 2009). The authoritative military history of the period is Piero Pieri, *Il Rinascimento e la crisi militare italiana* (Turin: Einaudi, 1952). The canonical source from the period itself is, of course, Francesco Guicciardini, *Storia d'Italia* (Turin: Einaudi, 1970), Book 1.

[2] Riccardo Fubini, "Lega italica e 'politica dell'equilibrio' all'avvento di Lorenzo de' Medici al potere," in *Italia Quattrocentesca: Politica e diplomazia nell'età di Lorenzo il Magnifico* (Milan: FrancoAngeli, 1994): 185-219.

[3] Pellegrini, *Le guerre d'Italia*, 59-60.

to avoid this was to bring in neutral, outside administrators all factions could agree on to handle local affairs in a supposedly impartial manner. Known as the podestà system, this odd method of running a government began to be common by the late 13th century, but this administration would need troops of its own and naturally hired outsiders, often non-Italians, to keep the peace.

Thus was born the *condottieri* (singular *condottiero* or *condottiere*). Meaning "contractor," it referred not only to the captains of mercenary bands but was also used as a general term for all the mercenaries in Italy during the Late Middle Ages and Renaissance. These flamboyant figures, sometimes of noble birth, had at their command experienced armies who hired themselves out to the highest bidder and kept to a strict code of professional ethics. Their fighting prowess and prestige soon put them in high demand, and rulers all across Italy eagerly bid for their services. Even the Vatican hired them as the Papal States sought to expand their influence in one of Italy's most militant periods.

Inevitably, having so much influence meant that the *condottieri* became a major power in their own right, wheeling and dealing in the incredibly complex and cutthroat world of Italian politics. They also made some interesting innovations into the practice of war and revolutionized the place of the mercenary in society.

The Condottieri: The History of Italy's Elite Mercenaries during the Middle Ages and Renaissance examines the companies' origins, and the important roles they played in the history of Italy. Along with pictures of important people, places, and events, you will learn about the *condottieri* like never before.

The Rise of Mercenary Companies

While mercenaries have existed since the early days of civilization, Italy would bring about a significant shift in the number of mercenaries needed and how they were hired around the 14th century. The city-states of Venice, Genoa, and Florence, being the richest, were the first to start hiring mercenary bands, and Venice was a prime example of why the need for mercenaries was so pressing.

As Venice found its footing in international trade in the 9th century, it had to deal with the geopolitics surrounding it, and despite its famous moniker, early Venice was by no means "serene." Following the founding of Venice came decades of internal political struggle as the Venetians disagreed amongst themselves about how to handle ties with Byzantine authorities. In the early 9th century, in fact, a pair of brothers who served as Doge joined up with the Bishop of nearby Zara, and by tentatively allying themselves with the Holy Roman Emperor Charlemagne, for the first time in their history they staged an open rebellion against the Byzantines. This bought them a small amount of autonomy, but it also meant Venice was now caught between two powerful empires. The city needed to maintain a difficult balance in order to preserve autonomy, and even after some of its leaders worked with Charlemagne, Venetians at one point sought help from the Byzantines to keep Charlemagne from seizing too much control of their territory.

Thanks to savvy negotiations, Venice was able to strike a balance and benefit from its proximity to the two empires, at least insofar as the superpowers helped the city retain its independence from the Italian mainland. When the Lombard kingdom was absorbed by the Franks, Venice was able to reaffirm its connection to the Byzantine Empire.

A crucial moment came when Charlemagne and the Byzantine emperor went to war with one another, and Venice was able to reap the rewards of the peace treaty. The Pax Nicephori of 803 explicitly declared the Venetian dukedom to be a part of the Byzantine Empire, and Charlemagne, already in declining health, accepted the unfavorable terms without further fight. However, the Byzantine empire also suffered some losses in signing the treaty, so Venice was one of the few winners, gaining all of the political, cultural, and commercial benefits of the peace without losing its independence. The Venetians were technically still Byzantine citizens who all had Byzantine honorifics and funding, but following the Pax Nicephori, they began to perceive themselves as Venetians, and they felt beholden to the fellow Venetians who elected them into power. Indeed, after the Pax Nicephori, the Byzantine Empire never again seriously interfered with their politics, and as the Byzantines got caught up dealing with closer enemies in the east, the Venetians explicitly refused to accept a subordinate position to any of the Germanic tribal kings who still held any power in Europe.

Another major benefit of the city's position between the two empires is that they were able to avoid falling into the feudal system that was a common practice in Lombardy and Tuscany. Instead, they were able to develop their own form of mixed government that served them well, and they avoided falling into the seemingly endless wars of Guelf against Ghibelline that continued on and off throughout the peninsula for years and caused substantial economic setbacks to those involved. For the remainder of the 9th century, the Republic was on a major upwards swing.

In fact, by being independent but being in the middle of everything, the Republic of Venice was able to acquire an ideal position by playing the role of intermediary, both in terms of politics and commerce. Furthermore, in addition to being the main middleman of international sea trade, Venice was also a major exporter of timber and glass, and by the 13th century, glass manufacturing had become another of the city's major industries. The artisans behind the glass-making wizardry were respected members of society, their offspring often marrying into the richest of the rich in the community. Glass artisans were urged to keep their unique glass-making techniques within their families. Keeping the secrets of various trades within the borders only added another edge to the rising power of Venice.

In the 1370s, Venetian craftsmen introduced an improved version of the medieval bombard, which were archaic cannons that expelled balls of stone or steel. From then on, all local naval fleets were outfitted with bombards. A fraction of the arsenal's craftsmen were also assigned to build early models of guns to be used in the Genoese conflicts later on.

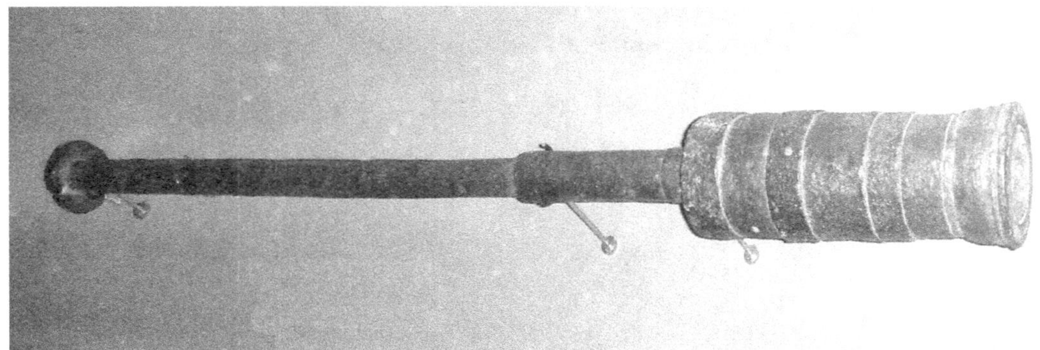

A 14th century bombard

Meanwhile, by the end of the 12th century, the Genoese colonial and commercial system had its principal elements firmly in place. Thanks to a comprehensive network of ships that were able to reach every part of the Mediterranean, the city developed and was in control of numerous thriving merchant colonies which had trading privileges in the East. To go along with this newfound power, the Genoese were not reluctant to use force to impose their will, which enabled them to open new markets, maintain their current routes, and establish trading outposts.[4]

Due to this strategy, by the end of the 13th century, the Republic of Genoa had founded colonies all around the Black Sea and the Sea of Azov, as well as in the Aegean, and on Cyprus.[5]

---

[4] Kirk, 10.

It also was able to establish further merchant colonies on the Iberian Peninsula as well as in England and in Flanders. Contrary to what one might imagine when thinking about a colonial relationship, in the case of Genoa, the relationship between the colony and the mother city was often rather flexible, albeit not because of any largesse on the part of the Republic. Instead, it was because the reach of the empire was so expansive that stricter control was virtually impossible. Although merchants sought to maintain contact across the empire, the element that held the whole system together was the fleet of Genoese ships. At this time, there still was almost no contact via inland methods; even in surrounding Liguria, no roads linked the various Genoese coastal towns, but instead, only maritime routes.[6]

Due to the complexity of its trade networks, it is impossible to characterize the mercantile practices of the Genoese people in one single way. Historians have settled on the concept of an "emporium," which works to describe a gateway to trade whose main goal was economic success, rather than control of new territories (as would be the case in a "colonial" enterprise").[7] The three most important eastern trade destinations for Genoa were Oltremare, Alexandria, and Romania.[8] To the south, the Genoese traded with North Africa, all the way from Tunis in the west to Bougie, Ceuta, and Safi on the Atlantic. Sicily, Naples, and Sardinia were all risky ventures for Genoa in the Late Middle Ages due to their conflicts with other regional powers, including the Vatican and the Pisan Empire.[9] In their own neighborhood, Genoa also traded with Provence and Champagne, particularly in cloth, but this relationship was rocky because it depended on whether Genoa was in a state of war or peace with France.[10]

---

[5] See Evgeny Khvalkov, *The Colonies of Genoa in the Black Sea Region: Evolution and Transformation.* (London: Routledge, 2017).

[6] Kirk, 10-11. One exception is in the case of Corsica, where the Genoese were able to penetrate into the interior— but it took them centuries to do so, particularly because the Genoese were often at war with Pisa over control of Corsica.

[7] Catia Brilli, *Genoese Trade and Migration in the Spanish Atlantic, 1700–1830* (Cambridge, UK: Cambridge University Press, 2016), 6. On the problems defining Genoa's status, see also Airaldi, *Genova e Liguria Nel Medioevo.*

[8] Epstein, 141.

[9] Epstein, 143.

[10] Epstein, 144.

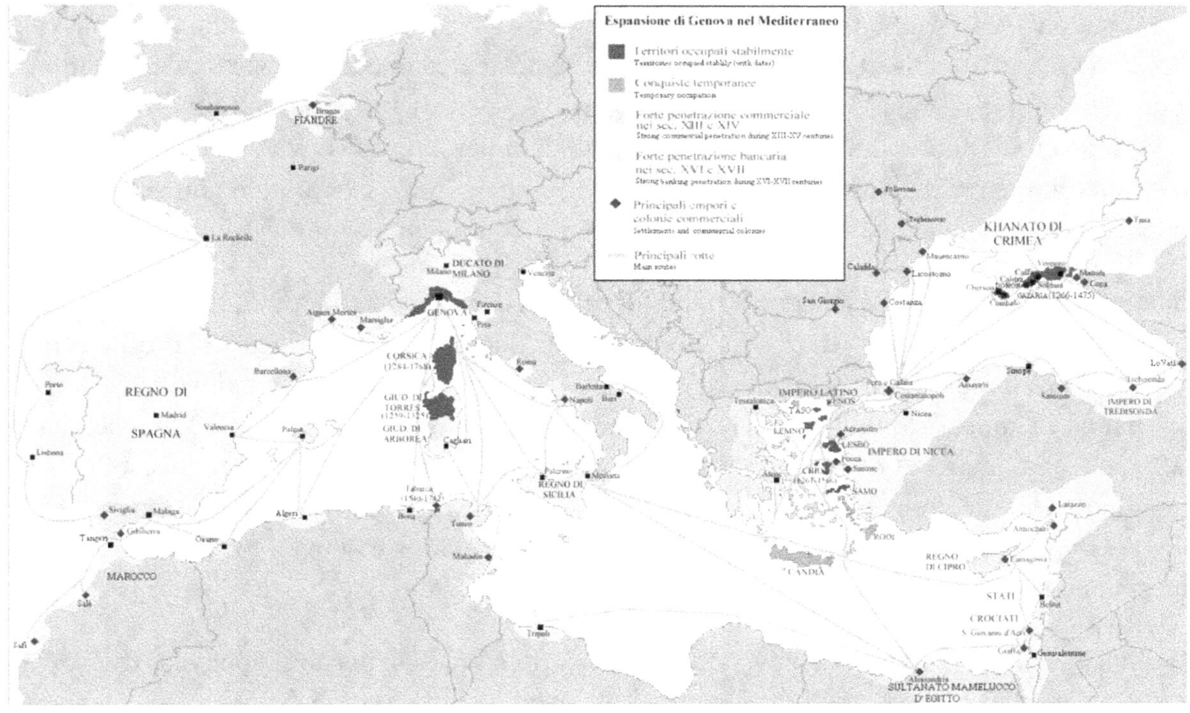

A map of Genoan spheres of influence at the end of the 14ᵗʰ century

On the one hand, Genoa in the Late Middle Ages was dynamic and robust, providing a fertile ground for some of its most promising endeavors to take root, but there was also a dark side, because as the most powerful families of Genoa began to prosper in its developing empire, society also tended to become more clannish. With that, the Genoese began to earn a richly deserved reputation for being backstabbers. The city broke into multiple fiefdoms that represented the individual clans, and one example of these rivalries still visible today is the dense concentration of towers that crowd the city, each one taller than the next. The towers became sites of fighting, and competing fiefdoms would go to great lengths to destroy each other's towers. In order to stop the constant chaos, in 1196 the city had to impose a limit on the height of the towers, and authorities threatened the destruction of towers as a punishment for bad behavior.[11]

At the same time, Florence operated as a *comuni*, or municipal commune. General assemblies – which were essentially forums attended by Florentines of all classes – were conducted at least 4 times every year. A council consisting of 150 officials was formed and entrusted with all legislative responsibilities. On the tier above them was the executive body, which was a board seated with 12 consuls – a pair each from the six Florentine districts at the time. Consuls, who were typically from the nobility, served a maximum term of 1 year each, and the consuls worked in rotation. A set of two consuls from the same district ruled the *comuni* for two months at a time.

---

[11] Walton, 18.

Banking businesses took the Florentine industries by storm. The popularization of what came to be known as the "bills of exchange," which were postdated cheques of sorts, was what facilitated the rise of the Florentine banking industry. Not only were these multipurpose IOU and convertible credit hybrids recognized in almost all commercial zones, which boosted foreign trade and eliminated the hassle of lugging around cumbersome sacks of gold and silver currencies, they allowed bankers to squeeze through loopholes to avoid usury laws.

The most compelling consequence of the Florentine banking takeover was the birth of capitalism, an economical system wherein private owners pulled the strings and profited from a city or nation's industries from behind the scenes. Bankers were relatively uninvolved, keeping their hands clean, sullied only by the metallic scent of the florin, as the hands of the merchants, craftsmen, and laborers underneath them turned rough and calloused. Injecting investments and providing loans – with interest – to the local Florentine businesses was about the extent of their role, yet they soared to the top of the pyramid, enjoying salaries that even the highest-paid statesmen could only dream of having.

At this point, the Florentine elites, populated by minted merchants and moneyed, land-owning knights, were the smallest of all the classes. Still, even with the establishment of the General and Executive Councils, the aristocracy continued to hold considerable power and could even overrule decisions made by the councils in certain cases. This system of governance was a variant of the oligarchy, wherein a small group of nobility ruled over the masses, but it also meant there was constant domestic unrest. As such, the environment was ideal for the reliance on mercenaries.

Across these city-states, a practice came about to sign a *condotta* (contract) with mercenaries, and the mercenaries were represented by their contracted leader, who came to be known as the *"Condottiere."* Of course, there had been mercenaries before this time, but they had tended to be foreigners often returning from the Crusades, and they could be considered as much bandits as hired swords. Some of the first bands to rise above this and show a bit of professionalism were the Ventura Companies, led by Duke Werner von Urslingen and Count Konrad von Landau, two Germans. Werner impressed potential employers by keeping his men in line with rigid discipline. His troops assented to this because the contracts he negotiated gave them an equal division of the spoils. At its height, the Ventura Company numbered around 3,000 *barbute* (a *barbuta* was made up of a knight and a sergeant) and became known as "the Great Company."

Foreigners continued to make up the bulk of mercenaries in the 14th century, the greatest numbers being English, Germans, Swiss, Catalans, and French. A large influx of English arrived after 1360, when the Treaty of Brétigny ended the first phase of the Hundred Years' War. Italians wouldn't become the majority of hired swords in their own land until the end of that century.

The most prominent of these foreign mercenary leaders was John Hawkwood (c. 1323-1394).

Born the son of a gentleman landowner in England, he signed on as a longbowman in the army of King Edward III during the Hundred Years' War, but after the Battle of Poitiers in 1356, he joined the White Company of mercenaries and moved into Italy to seek his fortune. Also called the Great Company or the English Company, this was the best mercenary company of its day. Hawkwood rose in the ranks to end up as its captain in 1363.

An engraving that depicts Hawkwood

One of his first important battles came on July 28 of the following year. At that time, Hawkwood was working for the Republic of Pisa, which was fighting the Republic of Florence, and initially Hawkwood enjoyed some victories, but then the Florentines assembled a larger army and clashed with his at the town of Cascina, a few miles from Pisa. Hawkwood had around 800 Englishmen with him and 4,000 levies from Pisa of mediocre quality. Facing him were 4,000 knights and 11,000 infantry under the Italian *condottiero* Galeotto I Malatesta (1299–1385).

Malatesta marched his troops toward Pisa to threaten the city and Hawkwood decided to make a stand near the town of Cascina. It was a sweltering day, and Malatesta, who had fallen ill, ordered an early stop. While he convalesced in his tent, many of his men removed their armor and went to bathe in the Arno River. No one thought to post a guard on the camp or put out vedettes. Hawkwood's scouts reported the situation, and since he knew he faced faced superior numbers, the Englishman decided to take the Florentines by surprise.

The road to the camp, however, was longer than Hawkwood realized, and by the time he got near, the Florentines had belatedly sent out an advanced party of cavalry and about 500 Genoese crossbowmen to guard the road. Hawkwood waited until the sun was low and in the eyes of the enemy. The wind was in his favor too, blowing dust in their faces.

The Pisans managed to break through the Florentine vanguard and reach their camp, but the Florentines sent cavalry circling around the smaller force to hit the Pisan baggage train. The Genoese crossbowmen seemed to be everywhere, firing from cover at the Pisan force. The English knights, boiling in their armor, were meeting stiff resistance in the Florentine camp and began to flag. Hawkwood ordered a retreat, and he and his knights rode away, leaving the Pisan infantry to its fate. Some 2,000 of them surrendered. Casualties on both sides are otherwise unclear.

While a defeat, the Battle of Cascina demonstrated Hawkwood's tactical mastery. He had been able to hold his own with a numerically inferior force that according to some accounts wasn't nearly as well trained as that of his foe. He had also seized an opportunity for surprise and used the terrain and weather to his advantage. His reputation grew, and the many battles that followed in his career were usually victories.

Hawkwood and his Great Company would later serve Pope Gregory XI (r. 1370-1378), but when the Vatican refused to pay him on time, the mercenary captain decided to loot his way through Tuscany, where the city-states were already political rivals to the pope because they objected to the Papal States' expansion in central Italy. He plundered churches and villages and extorted money from local leaders to get him to leave. The city-states thought Pope Gregory XI was behind the raids, which some historians believe was indeed the case. Florence formed a league with Milan and Siena and declared war on the Papal States, a war later called the War of the Eight Saints that lasted from 1375-1378.

A medieval depiction of the coronation of Pope Gregory XI

The league's first move was to encourage rebellion of areas already occupied by the Papal States, and more than 40 cities, including important ones such as Bologna and Perugia, rose up against the Vatican's rule. Naturally, this gave Hawkwood plenty of work to do. When Città di Castello, nominally under the Papal States, rebelled against the pope, Hawkwood went there to put down the rebellion. While Gregory only wanted him to achieve a quick victory followed by submission, the mercenary took the city and said he would not return it until the pontiff had paid what he owed. Not having sufficient funds, Gregory instead awarded him the city itself.

The Vatican had another weapon besides an army of English mercenaries. Pope Gregory XI excommunicated everyone in the Florentine government and put the city-state under interdict, meaning that religious services could not be performed there. He also declared that anyone in Europe was free to seize the property of the many Florentine merchants who had set up businesses in other countries. This had a massive impact on the city-state's economy, and in response, Florence dismantled the Inquisition, repealed usury laws, and formed its own religious societies and processions. When this wasn't enough to assuage the populace's worries, the Florentine government forced the clergy to perform church rites. It also seized a large amount of church property to pay for the coming war and shore up the economy.

During the conflict, the English mercenary captain did not actually fight in Tuscany, as the Florentines had paid him 130,000 florins plus a large annual stipend not to attack. Instead Hawkwood limited himself to putting down rebellions in the Papal States. Pope Gregory XI, who lacked any sizeable force aside from Hawkwood's, could do nothing but fume.

In February 1377, Hawkwood marched on the town of Cesena, another of the municipalities in revolt. The papal representative there, Cardinal Robert of Geneva, had a garrison of Breton mercenaries to keep order. There had been a shortage of food that winter and that had led to clashes between the *condottieri* and the local populace, who complained that the foreign soldiers got to stuff themselves while they starved. The clashes became violent and several of the cardinal's men were killed.

While making public statements that he would try to solve the food situation, Robert secretly sent word for Hawkwood and Italian *condottiero* Alberico da Barbiano to bring their men to town. On the night of February 2, 1377, they struck when some of the cardinal's men opened the town gates and the *condottieri* rushed inside. A brutal night of murder, rape, and pillage ensued. Even religious sites were ransacked and clergy killed. The streets were piled with dead bodies, hundreds of women were carried off, and a Breton soldier discovered a child hiding under the altar of the church of San Antonio del Campo Boario. He dragged the boy out, killed him, and left his body on the altar.

A portrait of Alberico da Barbiano

The actions disgusted Hawkwood, who had objected to the orders to attack, but the events certainly struck struck fear in the other cities, and that same year, another mercenary army raised by the pope managed to take Bologna.

After the sack of Cesena, Hawkwood changed sides. Pope Gregory XI died the following year, and one of his successors was none other than Cardinal Robert of Geneva, who took the name Clement VII (r. 1378-1394) after being named by the cardinals in France. He took up office in Avignon because another pope, Urban VI (r. 1378-1389), had been elected in Rome. This caused a schism in the Church, with one pope in Rome and another "antipope" in Avignon. The schism wasn't healed until 1417. Urban VI negotiated a peace treaty with Florence. In return for lifting the excommunication and interdict, Florence had to pay Rome 200,000 florins, repeal all laws against the church offices, and restore stolen church property.

Clement VII

Hawkwood was the quintessential mercenary, loyal only to his own interests but also a brave and cunning warrior. When a friar once greeted him with the saying, "May God give you peace," he replied, "Do you not know that I live by war and that peace would ruin me?" It turned out he need not worry, because Hawkwood was proof that a man could make a major fortune as a *condottiero*. His annual salary varied widely depending on the phase of his career and the fortunes of war, but it ranged between 6,000 and 80,000 florins at a time when the skilled Florentine craftsmen who made that city such a jewel of art and architecture only made 30 florins a year. And this was only the official pay. Furthermore, there is little doubt Hawkwood received a large share of loot on campaign and bribes and extra fees under the table. A regular *condottiero* made much less, but even so, the life of a mercenary was a profitable one.

Hawkwood also trained a generation of fighting men, many of whom rose to prominence. One of them was Alberico da Barbiano (c. 1344–1409), an Italian son of a noble family in Romagna. He was said to have felt a great amount of guilt over the Cesena Bloodbath and decided to leave Hawkwood to form a company of only Italians. Called the *Compagnia di San Giorgio* ("St.

George Company"), he started with only 200 men, but his numbers soon swelled to 4,000. He worked hard to train his men and improve cavalry tactics, and the company became so successful that it began to edge out the foreign companies.

In 1379, he was hired by Pope Urban VI to fight against Antipope Clement VII, who had ordered the Cesena Bloodbath. Alberico da Barbiano crushed the antipope's Breton troops near Rome on June 29, 1379, which helped assuage the mercenary's guilt over his part in the massacre.

Interestingly, this was not the first Company of St. George in Italy. Another early company was that of Lodrisio Visconti, who formed a Company of St. George in 1339, but it was a short-lived enterprise. That same year, it was destroyed at the Battle of Parabiago by Luchino Visconti, Lodrisio's uncle, who led the forces of Milan and handed the new company a complete defeat.

Thanks to the second, more successful Company of St. George, Italian *condottieri* rapidly rose in demand and prestige to dominate the military affairs of Italy. Italians preferred them over foreigners because they shared a language, and often the *condottieri* were enmeshed in local family and political networks, making them a more familiar quantity. That said, this did not make them more reliable, because Italian politics constantly consisted of nasty backstabbing, and never more so than during the Renaissance. The mercenary captains drove hard bargains, always knowing they could find work elsewhere, and many rose to prominence in local politics, thereby becoming potential rivals to the very people who hired them.

On the other hand, they brought a new level of professionalism to warfare. The era regenerated interest in antiquity, and the *condottieri* studied Roman military manuals to learn how the greatest ancient empire managed to defeat its enemies. This led some mercenary captains to incorporate sophisticated tactics into their fighting, quite unlike the set-piece battles the more traditional knights preferred.

Condottieri companies often found themselves fighting each other, such as at the Battle of Castagnaro on March 11, 1387. On one side was the army of Verona under Giovanni del Ordelaffi, and on the other was the army of Padua led by Hawkwood, who had at his command 7,000 mounted men-at-arms, 1,000 infantry, 600 mounted English longbowmen, and a few bombards. After unsuccessfully besieging Verona, Hawkwood moved out of the area and Ordelaffi's force followed him with 9,000 mounted men-at-arms, 2,600 crossbowmen and pikemen, and a large number of poorly trained militia. He also had 24 bombards and three multi-barreled *ribaudiaux*. Also called "organ guns," these were carts with a row of small cannons on them that could be fired one after another to great effect against infantry and cavalry at close range. However, it seems the artillery lagged behind and didn't make it to the battle on time, a common occurrence with the cumbersome early artillery pieces trying to make their way over primitive roads.

Hawkwood, realizing he was outnumbered, took up a defensive position in keeping with English practice during the Hundred Years' War. He arrayed his forces behind an irrigation drain flooded by recent rains, and to his left were marshes and to his right was an irrigation canal flowing into the River Adige. Most of his men were positioned unmounted behind the irrigation ditch, with some cavalry and the mounted longbowmen kept as a mobile reserve.

The Veronese first tried a frontal infantry assault, with men bearing bundles of reeds to fill up the ditch. The first assault failed, but the second gained a foothold. Both sides committed their second lines, but the Veronese enjoyed greater numbers and inexorably pushed the Paduans back from the ditch.

Hawkwood realized that he no longer enjoyed the advantage of terrain, but he also saw Ordelaffi's entire force was engaged except for a few reserve cavalry and the ragged militia. Thus, he sent his mobile reserve, along with the Paduan crossbowmen and handgonners on his far right, in a flanking movement through a path he had already scouted. The Paduans fell on the Veronese left and took them completely by surprise. As they released a volley into the Veronese front line, the Veronese advance stopped abruptly in confusion, and the Paduan main line took this opportunity to push forward. With that, the Veronese began to fall back in disarray, and Hawkwood then rushed at the Veronese reserve and captured it with barely a fight. Most of the militia simply ran, except for one detachment that vowed to fight until the last man. Their morale was greater than their training and armament, however, and they didn't last long.

In the end, the Paduans captured 4,600 men-at-arms and 800 infantry. The chronicles relate that a total of 716 men were killed in the battle, with only about 100 of them being from the Paduan side.

The Contract

Mercenary companies soon developed a standard operating procedure for their business that the city-states could accept. The contract stipulated the pay and term of service, as well as other details such as supply and where the troops would be billeted.

If the city-state decided not to renew, one of the main stipulations in the contract was that a mercenary company could not fight against that city-state for two years. This increased trust between the two sides and eliminated the practice seen in some parts of Europe of an enemy bribing away a mercenary company with a higher fee.

Payment usually came in the form of an advance followed by regular installments. Provisions were generally supplied when on campaign in friendly territory, with the expectation that the *condottieri* would live off the land once they entered enemy territory. When in billets, the mercenaries could usually buy their food at a discount. Anything taken in enemy territory was the property of the *condottieri*, as were the arms and equipment of defeated enemies. Any captured land or buildings, of course, became the property of the employer. Bonuses were paid to those who got injured or disabled in battle, or who showed exceptional bravery. The best fighters might even be offered citizenship.

In early contracts, pay was given to the captain for disbursement to the men, but corrupt captains often skimmed the money and claimed the client hadn't given the full sum, causing all sorts of problems. To avoid this, in later contracts the pay was distributed directly to each man, and while this made more work for the client, it saved him from many headaches.

The *condottieri* company, in turn, had to be of a certain size and show up fully equipped and trained for their new job. They had to obey the orders of the city-state government and, when ordered, launch into a campaign without delay.

Billets were generally arranged in a fortified camp outside the city walls. No employer wanted a bunch of rough and tumble mercenaries living in town, and many contracts specifically forbade them from entering any friendly walled settlement without express permission. While the contracts stipulated that the *condottieri* be law abiding in friendly territory and not abuse the citizens, it was best to be on the safe side. This became standard procedure for other mercenary companies in other nations, such as the German Landsknechts used across the Holy Roman Empire.

At the same time, it was in the best interest of the mercenary band to stick to the agreement. Italy was not that big of a region (one could not call it a country until the 19th century), and dishonest dealing by a *condottieri* captain would soon ensure that he would never work again.

The *condottieri* generally served loyally as long as they were paid, but they were not the most eager of fighters, and there was always a concern that a city-state could fall behind on payment. Unlike knights who fought for honor and glory, the mercenary fought for money and loot, and he did not want to risk his hide unnecessarily. In addition, the *condottieri* captains were generally acquainted with one another. They could be friends or, at least, professional colleagues, which led to a somewhat implicit understanding that their battles should not be too bloody. There was much sound and fury, much maneuvering and counter-maneuvering, but many battles of the time were more imitations of battles than the real thing. Once one side had outmaneuvered the other or caused the vanguard of the other to give ground, the proceedings often came to an abrupt halt. Then one side would "surrender" and everyone would come to amicable terms. This must have rubbed the egos of the leading Italian families raw, but there was little they could do. Besides, the terms of surrender were never too onerous. One had to keep all potential clients happy, after all.

Contracts were overseen by a go-between hired by the state called a *collaterali*. Later in the period, as some powerful *condottieri* became de facto rulers of certain city-states, the role of the *collaterali* expanded to include making sure the army was supplied and paid, and the job became a permanent one. It was his job to make sure the *condottieri* were fully equipped and following orders, and they could fine units and individuals found to be deficient. They maintained discipline in camp with a small group of their own tough fighters. Some *collaterali* even had their own executioners on staff.

Arms and Armor

A 15th century depiction of a *condottiero*

Diego Velazquez's painting of *condottiero* Ambrogio Spinola

The period of the *condottieri*, which lasted from roughly 1300-1500, witnessed great changes in weapons and armor, and for the most part the mercenaries kept up with these changes.

The backbone of any *condottieri* army was the heavy cavalry, many of them knights. At the beginning of the period they did not generally have full plate armor. Most would have a breast and backplate, helmet, and the rest of the body was protected with chainmail. This type of armor, made up of connected links of metal backed by padded garments, proved good protection against bladed weapons and, to a lesser extent, stabbing weapons. But even with a layer of padding behind it, the wearer could get seriously injured by a strong hit. A mace could crack bones without ever piercing the armor, and even a strong sword blow could cause terrible bruising, fractures, or breaks. Some warriors wore their chainmail over a suit of brigandine, a shirt with metal plates sewn or riveted onto a cloth backing.

In the early period, arms and legs could be covered with chainmail or with fittings of leather molded to look like metal armor. Leather armor was much lighter and cooler than metal armor, although of course not nearly as strong. Often men wore a combination of chainmail and leather backed with a layer of quilted padding. Leather armor was generally *cuir bouilli*—boiled leather. Leather would be placed in boiling water which made it elastic and pliable and it was then hammered into shape as it shrank, thickened, and hardened. Each piece could be hammered into its proper shape much like metal to create a full suit of armor. The 14th century French chronicler Jean Froissart said that *cuir bouilli* was, "leather that no iron can pierce" and while that certainly was an overstatement, leather armor offered good protection.

As was always the case in military history, offense began to outpace defense. Crossbows grew more powerful and could pierce weaker armor, while the constant abuse from swords and axes in a melee would wear down leather or chainmail. Thus, full plate armor began to be developed. Plate armor became popular in early 14th century and grew in use until the development of the firearm made it obsolete in the 16th. Throughout the period, armor went through countless developments as armorers tried to better protect their clients and vied with one another in making the strongest and most visually appealing suits of armor. It should be remembered, however, that most of the surviving suits of armor were for the very rich. Many men rode into battle wearing suits made of iron rather than steel, and the steel could be of varying quality. A full suit of plate wasn't always the protection it was advertised to be.

Full plate was also fairly heavy, so it was best if the wearer stayed on horseback, but this is not to say that plate armor was too cumbersome. Images of knights being lifted onto their horses by crane are Hollywood fiction. Modern experiments with accurate replicas of period armor, and records from the period itself, show that men could walk around, mount horses, fight, and even manage a sort of lumbering jog. The real problem with plate armor was the lack of visibility from the enclosed helm and the heat that would build up inside. Indeed, the history of the *condottieri* is full of stories of armored men dying simply as a result of the hot Italian summer.

In the earlier part of the period, a fully armored horseman would often carry a shield, but this was eventually discarded as full plate armor came into vogue.

Armored horsemen were usually armed with a lance and a sword, and they would move in tight formation, knee to knee with the men by their side to create a terrifying wall of lances and steel men. Even the horses would often be given metal armor called barding.

Next down the ladder, the men-at-arms were well armed and armored as well, and may often have been indistinguishable from the knights except for a lack of a heraldic crest on their shield. They could fight on foot or on horseback. The poorer among them, or those from smaller companies, might not have worn a full plate even in the later part of the period, although all would aspire to both for reasons of status and safety.

The archers of a *condottieri* army could either be actual bowmen or, more often, crossbowmen. Hawkwood used English longbowmen who could shoot at a much faster rate of fire than a crossbow, but the Italians favored crossbows because they took less training than a bow and were quite powerful, able to punch through all but the heaviest armor at close range. They were used effectively by all *condottieri* armies and tipped the balance in numerous engagements. Only in the earliest period were longbows found with any frequency in *condottieri* armies.

Condottieri armies also made use of a new military technology—the cannon. The first record of a cannon in Europe comes from a manuscript written in 1326 which has an illustration showing an armored man with what looks like a slow match lighting a vase-shaped object that fires a large arrow. This crude device was quickly replaced with a new type of cannon in the form of a large cylinder made up of iron bars fused together and strengthened with hoops like a barrel. In fact, this is where the term for the "barrel" of a gun comes from. These devices were called *cannons* or *bombards*. The arrow was replaced with a sphere of stone or lead, both materials being cheap and easy to work. These cannon balls proved to be more aerodynamic and generated more impact than the old-style arrows.

Cannons were quickly brought into use both for sieges and pitched battles. The earliest reference to cannons being used in sieges was the Siege of Friuli in Italy in 1331. They were too heavy and cumbersome to be used much in the field, but this eventually changed by the middle of the 15th century. Gunpowder became more powerful, and thus cannon barrels could be made smaller and lighter. These more portable barrels were placed on a wooden bed with an axle and a pair of wheels. A wooden trail made the third point of contact with the ground, and acted as a hitch for a team of horses. The barrel could be elevated or depressed using a trunnion, a pivot that allowed the barrel to move up or down and then be held in place with a metal rod through holes in a metal frame. In fact, the artillery used in the year 1500 looked much like that used in the Napoleonic Wars or the American Civil War.

The 15th century saw an increasing number of handgonners. The handgonne first appeared in the 14th century, and was the first crude black powder infantry weapon, basically a smaller version of the early cannons. Indeed, the term "hand cannon" is still used for large firearms to this day. The handgonnes were simple affairs, with a short iron barrel and touchhole that would be filled with black powder, wadding and a stone or lead bullet. The barrel had a simple wooden stock, basically a short pole, that the handgonner tucked under his arm. He used the other hand to light the touchhole with the slow match. Such an awkward firing stance made aiming difficult, plus the short smoothbore wasn't ever going to guarantee much accuracy anyway. Modern experiments have proven, however, that a handgonne had better penetrative power at close range than any other medieval ranged weapon.

Later, a simple lever device that held the slow match, called a serpentine, was developed. Pressing the level brought the slow match down on the firing pan. This way the handgonner could aim down the barrel although at some risk to his eyes. Some early handgonnes have a notch or bead at the end to aid in aiming.

The serpentine was soon replaced with an actual trigger and the soldier was able to properly bring the gun up to his shoulder and look down the barrel, vastly improving the soldier's ability to aim. This gun was called the arquebus, and it was the first black powder firearm that looked like a modern rifle although the inside of the barrel remained a smoothbore. Rifling was not developed until the 16th century and did not become commonplace until the 19th century.

The arquebus appeared by the end of the 15th century, at the very end of the *condottieri* period. In 1482, when the army of Milan marched to war, it included only 233 crossbowmen as compared to 1,200 handgonners. The Papal States even had mounted arquebusiers in the 1490s, and as events would soon demonstrate, such an effective firearm would help sound the death knell for the *condottieri*'s heavily armored cavalry.

Crossbowmen and handgonners were the lowest in the hierarchy of *condottieri* armies, and tended to have less armor. They might wear *cuir bouilli* or chainmail or a jerkin of brigandine. The lucky ones perhaps had a breastplate. Generally they wore open helms or pot helms rather than the fully enclosed helmets of the knights and men-at-arms. These cheaper helmets offered less protection but gave more visibility, vital to the function of a crossbowman or handgonner.

As time went on, infantry played an increasingly large role in the fighting. They never entirely supplanted the heavy cavalry, but dismounted men-at-arms, crossbowmen, and handgonners became more visible and important. Heavy infantry armed with polearms proved especially effective at unseating mounted knights, although the *condottieri* never adopted the pike squares of the Swiss or Landsknecht mercenaries.

It is important to remember that while the *condottieri* were the main mercenaries in Italy during this period, others appeared as well, such as the Swiss and the German-speaking Landsknecht. There were also Spaniards who wielded a sword and buckler and acted as light infantry. Then there were the *stradiotti*, light cavalry from the Balkans who were effective scouts and skirmishers and much feared for their penchant for brutality against civilians. Armed with lances, bows, and crossbows, they proved quite effective against armed opponents too. Some city-states even hired Turks, and the demand for fighting men was so high that all of these kinds of warriors could be found in Italy at a given time.

Tactics

A *condottieri* army on campaign was a large and complex organization. A strict hierarchy of command was vital, as was a good quartermaster system and a well-stocked baggage train. While in enemy territory, the army would live off the land as much as possible, but a wise commander would bring food stores along in case the pickings were lean. Peasants would flee to the woods at the approach of any army, taking all their portable stock with them. Much time could be wasted on the march hunting down these bands of fugitives, and while in hostile territory, one didn't want to break up one's army too much in the search of provisions.

The Italian mercenary armies were known to be good at organization. As the French chronicler Philippe de Commynes admitted, "As for the provision of food supplies and other things necessary for maintaining an army in the field, they do it much better than we do."

In addition to military command and a quartermaster system, a *condottieri* army would also bring along one or more chaplains. This might seem odd considering that the mercenaries were known for their violent ways and thought nothing of looting churches and monasteries in enemy lands, but the average person in the period was deeply superstitious and would not want to go into battle without a blessing. It appears the men compartmentalized their faith, thinking it necessary to pray to God to defeat the enemy so one could loot God's house later.

The army also brought along barber-surgeons. These individuals did everything from cutting hair to removing arrows, and were often self-trained or came up through an apprenticeship with a similarly unqualified barber-surgeon. Attempts would be made to cauterize or stitch wounds and wrap them in bandages, but in cases of depressed fractures, internal bleeding, or damage to internal organs, the prognosis was not good. It also didn't help that these well-meaning amateurs didn't understand the germ theory of disease, and thus didn't wash their hands before treating their patients. Sadly, this basic precaution wasn't figured out until the 19th century.

Still, lighter wounds could generally be cared for, and there was some attempt at keeping camps clean and sanitary. Privies would be inspected, and the area was kept relatively clear of refuse to reduce the number of flies and other vermin. On campaign this wasn't as much of an issue since camp would be moved every night, but when billeted outside the client's city, the *condottieri* camp had to be kept in good order. One constant problem was venereal disease. As with armies throughout history, the *condottieri* attracted a large number of prostitutes who spread diseases that could only be "cured" with dubious herbal concoctions.

In one humorous episode, when the Paduans defeated the Venetians at the Battle of Brentelle in 1386 and captured their baggage train, they received 211 prostitutes in the bargain. Instead of being claimed as booty or abused like the local peasant women, they were treated well, given garlands of flowers, and invited to join the officers at breakfast back in Padua to celebrate the victory.

Many sources dismiss the *condottieri* as simplistic in their tactics, using only large masses of heavy cavalry to slam their way through the opposition. While this was often the case in the early 14th century, over time they developed more elaborate techniques. Indeed, company leaders became skilled tacticians with varying approaches to battle, and two important *condottieri* leaders established rival schools of thought: Muzio Attendolo (1369-1424), nicknamed "Sforza" ("force"), and Braccio da Montone (1368-1424).

A 15th century miniature of Muzio Attendolo Sforza

When he was still a young man, Attendolo was ploughing his father's field when a force of mercenaries rode by. The men told him they were looking for recruits, and so Attendolo stole a horse from his father and joined them. One suspects that many young men were scooped up in this manner.

Attendolo's emphasis was on a single, hard hit against the enemy. He was beloved by his men, and he demanded that they keep tight discipline. He would train them hard to mass into dense formations that could move as a unit over the battlefield. Both infantry and cavalry would mass together to strike at an enemy's weak point, breaking their line and thus bringing chaos to the opposing force.

These tactics were a more refined version of those of his mentor, Alberico da Barbiano (c. 1344-1409), who himself had learned the art of war from Hawkwood. While da Barbiano looked down on infantry as only useful for garrison duty, Attendolo's ideas were more advanced. Times were changing, the infantry was growing more powerful, and he saw them as a useful branch of the service to fight alongside the mounted men.

Attendolo was greatly successful as a *condottiero* and ended up with a couple of fiefdoms in southern Italy, granted to him by the Kingdom of Naples for his excellent service. His son, Francesco I Sforza (the nickname became a family name), eventually rose to be the Duke of Milan. The family had come a long way from ploughing a field in some rural backwater, and it had done so quite quickly.

Francesco Sforza

Braccio da Montone, who was active in the early 15th century, had different ideas. Da Montone came from minor nobility and decided to make his fortune on the battlefield. He preferred the use of heavy cavalry, not only because they were made up of high-status men like himself, but also because their better speed suited his purposes. He divided his heavy cavalry into separate squadrons that would sweep around the enemy searching for weak spots, often exploiting narrow gaps between enemy units. By keeping a tight command and control, he was able to move numerous units at the same time and have them go where they would do the most good. He also kept a reserve and fed his units into battle piecemeal. When one squadron charged into the fray, the previous one would withdraw in order to rest. This allowed him to keep fresh troops on the field at all times and brought him success in battles such as the one fought at Sant'Egidio on July 12, 1416. The day was hot and dusty, and by letting his squadrons regularly rest and refresh themselves back at camp while other squadrons were fighting, he was able to wear down his opponents. Then, in the late afternoon, he charged with his entire force, and the exhausted enemy buckled. Many had already left their line to drink at a nearby stream and weren't even there to witness their defeat.

Braccio da Montone

Both captains expected discipline and inspired loyalty, and both had plenty of personal battlefield experience. Given how chaotic a medieval battle could be, with all the dust kicked up by hundreds of horses, the limited visibility out of closed helms, the noise, and general confusion, units under these two commanders were able to keep a remarkable amount of cohesion. As a result, the commanders were generally able to bring their plans to fruition.

Many commanders viewed the battle from atop a *carroccio*, a cart on which the officers would stand in order to get a better view of the battlefield. Signals could be sent to the men via trumpets or messengers riding swift horses. A wise *condottieri* leader would not be seen to stay too much behind the lines, however, because many of the best led their men into battle, fighting alongside them to encourage them to greater acts of bravery.

While it was common for the *condottieri* to engage in raiding and pitched battles, sieges were a standard part of medieval warfare that the *condottieri* tried to avoid as much as possible. Not only did the long waiting period stuck outside the city or castle walls in inclement weather risk boredom, food shortages, and disease, but once the surrounding area had been looted, there was no other chance at booty. Also, until artillery became more developed over time, victory was by no means certain.

As a result, it was much better, once the enemy was cooped up inside the walls, to leave a small force to watch over them and send the bulk of the army to ravage the countryside. If the crop was ripe, it would be harvested and kept for the troops, or even sold back to the starving locals. If the crop was not yet ready, it would be destroyed along with the farms and villages. Often the defenders would beg for a peace treaty at this point in order to spare their lands, which could be profitable for the *condottieri* and would keep the client happy. It would also mean that the enemy would not be completely destroyed. The client would need to keep the mercenaries for another year to guard against vengeance attacks.

Of course, if a city or castle could be taken, it was quite a prize. For example, when Braccio da Montone took Bologna in 1416, he sold it back to the citizens for 82,000 florins.

The Glory Years

In the 15th century, the *condottieri* reached the peak of their influence. During this time, the majority of mercenaries were Italian, and the majority of their leaders were landless nobility, second sons, or those from decayed lineages who had lost their hereditary land. They were accustomed to leading men, were not intimidated by displays of wealth, and were more than comfortable handling negotiations in the sumptuous palaces of their clients. Some mercenary captains were even princes who, backed by their considerable fortunes, were able to go far in their careers. It was a profitable venture, and one that could reap political and social rewards as well. The mercenaries became increasingly embroiled in city-state politics, with the *condottieri* captains often rising to a high level of nobility themselves.

Moreover, the organization of the mercenary bands began to change. The old system of the barbuta was replaced with the *lancia*, which meant the smallest unit of the force went from two people (a knight and a sergeant) to three (a capo-lancia, a groom, and a boy) or five (mounted knight, squire, page, and two archers or men-at-arms). Five lancia made up a *posta*, and five poste made a *bandiera* (flag). There were regional variations with the organization of the units, and different companies would form up in different ways. Milan, for example, had a four-man lance, but all throughout, the emphasis remained on heavy cavalry, as it would until the end of the *condottieri* period.

It should be noted that in the five-man lance, all men could fight. The squire would be a knight in training and would often fight alongside the knight. The page, too, was learning how to use weapons even if he was quite young. The page or boy would also take care of many of the day-to-day duties of the camp and do such menial but vital tasks as building fortifications and fetching water and spare weapons for the fighting line, allowing the more senior men to focus on combat or getting some rest before battle. The men of the lance would, of course, be separated during a fight into their separate tasks, the archers going with the other archers and so on. As a basic unit of camp and pay, however, they stuck together.

The young men acting as servants in the *condottieri* army would, in exchange for dealing with all the menial tasks, get unparalleled training from experienced veterans. In the course of their duties, they would learn how to care for horses, put on armor, and learn from the older men's conversations how best to fight. They would also receive more formal training in the use of weapons. Many of these boys rose in the ranks to become *condottieri* leaders themselves.

The life of the *condottieri* must have been an attractive one to sons who would never inherit the family farm or business because they were not the eldest son in the family. Typically, the only thing they had to look forward to was a long apprenticeship to some master, or life in the Church. Adventure, excitement, and the chance of booty must have tempted many away from the career path his father had chosen for them, but they would soon discover that such a path was a lot of hard work. *Condottieri* also had to deal with the diseases and tedium of camp life, and the terrors of war. Still, in a rough age where few expected to enjoy an easy life, it must have been the better option for many.

While the fighting men were generally seasoned veterans, training would be ongoing. One had to stay fit and hone his reflexes, and it wasn't enough to simply throw a bunch of experienced men together and expect them to fight as a coherent unit. They had to train in maneuvers and get to know and rely on the men beside them.

The troops received plenty of practice in the field – after all, since *condottieri* were expensive and might cause trouble to the local citizenry who were unfortunate enough to live near their camp, it was in the employer's best interest to send them on campaign. Even if the situation wasn't favorable for a major offensive, it was still useful to send the troops just inside the enemy's territory so they could live off the enemy's land instead of the employer's own. This gave the men useful training in the field, allowed them to harass and weaken the enemy, and provided a way to let the *condottieri* take out any pent up frustrations on a target.

The use of *condottieri* on both sides occurred in the wars between Milan and a league of Italian states that included Florence, the Papal States, and Venice from 1423-1454. The fighting was covered by Machiavelli's *History of Florence*, in which the legendary political philosopher observed, "None of the principal states were armed with their own proper forces. Thus the arms of Italy were either in the hands of the lesser princes, or of men who possessed no state; for the minor princes did not adopt the practice of arms from any desire of glory, but for the acquisition of either property or safety. The others (those who possessed no state) being bred to arms from their infancy, were acquainted with no other art, and pursued war for emolument, or to confer honor upon themselves."

The great political commentator had little love for the mercenaries, and he criticized them harshly for their behavior at the Battle of Anghiari on June 29, 1440. This battle, fought between Milan and the league of states led by Florence, turned out to be more of an imitation of a battle than an actual battle. The League included about 4,000 troops from Florence, 4,000 from the Papal States, and 300 knights from Venice led by Micheletto Attendolo. Numbers for the Milanese force, led by Niccolò Piccinino, are unclear, but they were more numerous than the League's force.

Machiavelli described the battle in detail:

> "The Florentines, under their commissaries, had drawn together their forces, and being joined by those of the pope, halted at Anghiari, a castle placed at the foot of the mountains that divide the Val di Tavere from the Val di Chiane, distant four miles from the Borgo San Sepolcro, on a level road, and in a country suitable for the evolutions of cavalry or a battlefield. As the Signory had heard of the count's victory and the recall of Niccolo, they imagined that without again drawing a sword or disturbing the dust under their horses' feet, the victory was their own, and the war at an end, they wrote to the commissaries, desiring them to avoid an engagement, as Niccolo could not remain much longer in Tuscany.

> "These instructions coming to the knowledge of Piccinino, and perceiving the necessity of his speedy return, to leave nothing unattempted, he determined to engage the enemy, expecting to find them unprepared, and not disposed for battle. In this determination he was confirmed by Rinaldo, the Count di Poppi, and other Florentine exiles, who saw their inevitable ruin in the departure of Niccolo, and hoped, that if he engaged the enemy, they would either be victorious, or vanquished without dishonor.

> "This resolution being adopted, Niccolo led his army, unperceived by the enemy, from Citta di Castello to the Borgo, where he enlisted two thousand men, who, trusting the general's talents and promises, followed him in hope of plunder. Niccolo then led his forces in battle array toward Anghiari, and had arrived within two miles of the place, when Micheletto Attendulo observed great clouds of dust, and conjecturing at once, that it must be occasioned by the enemy's approach, immediately called the troops to arms. Great confusion prevailed in the Florentine camp, for the ordinary negligence and want of discipline were now increased by their presuming the enemy to be at a distance, and they were more disposed to fight

than to battle; so that everyone was unarmed, and some wandering from the camp, either led by their desire to avoid the excessive heat, or in pursuit of amusement. So great was the diligence of the commissaries and of the captain, that before the enemy's arrival, the men were mounted and prepared to resist their attack; and as Micheletto was the first to observe their approach, he was also first armed and ready to meet them, and with his troops hastened to the bridge which crosses the river at a short distance from Anghiari.

"Pietro Giampagolo, having previous to the surprise, filled up the ditches on either side of the road, and leveled the ground between the bridge and Anghiari, and Micheletto having taken his position in front of the former, the legate and Simoncino, who led the troops of the church, took post on the right, and the commissaries of the Florentines, with Pietro Giampagolo, their captain, on the left; the infantry being drawn up along the banks of the river. Thus, the only course the enemy could take, was the direct one over the bridge; nor had the Florentines any other field for their exertions, excepting that their infantry were ordered, in case their cavalry were attacked in flank by the hostile infantry, to assail them with their crossbows, and prevent them from wounding the flanks of the horses crossing the bridge. Micheletto bravely withstood the enemy's charge upon the bridge; but Astorre and Francesco Piccinino coming up, with a picked body of men, attacked him so vigorously, that he was compelled to give way, and was pushed as far as the foot of the hill which rises toward the Borgo d'Anghiari; but they were in turn repulsed and driven over the bridge, by the troops that took them in flank.

"The battle continued two hours, during which each side had frequent possession of the bridge, and their attempts upon it were attended with equal success; but on both sides of the river, the disadvantage of Niccolo was manifest; for when his people crossed the bridge, they found the enemy unbroken, and the ground being leveled, they could maneuver without difficulty, and the weary be relieved by such as were fresh. But when the Florentines crossed, Niccolo could not relieve those that were harassed, on account of the hindrance interposed by the ditches and embankments on each side of the road; thus whenever his troops got possession of the bridge, they were soon repulsed by the fresh forces of the Florentines; but when the bridge was taken by the Florentines, and they passed over and proceeded upon the road, Niccolo having no opportunity to reinforce his troops, being prevented by the impetuosity of the enemy and the inconvenience of the ground, the rear-guard became mingled with the van, and occasioned the utmost confusion and disorder; they were forced to flee, and hastened at full speed toward the Borgo.

"The Florentine troops fell upon the plunder, which was very valuable in horses, prisoners, and military stores, for not more than a thousand of the enemy's cavalry reached the town. The people of the Borgo, who had followed Niccolo in the hope of plunder, became booty themselves, all of them being taken, and obliged to pay a ransom. The colors and carriages were also captured. This victory was much more advantageous to the Florentines than injurious to the duke; for, had they been conquered, Tuscany would have been his own; but he, by his defeat, only lost the horses and accoutrements of his army, which could be replaced without any very serious expense. Nor was there ever an instance of wars being carried on in an enemy's country with less injury to the assailants than at this; for in so great a defeat, and in a battle which continued four hours, only one man died, and he, not from wounds inflicted by hostile weapons, or any honorable means, but, having fallen from his horse, was trampled to death. Combatants then engaged with little danger; being nearly all mounted, covered with armor, and preserved from death whenever they chose to surrender, there was no necessity for risking their lives; while fighting, their armor defended them, and when they could resist no longer, they yielded and were safe.

"This battle, from the circumstances which attended and followed it, presents a striking example of the wretched state of military discipline in those times. The enemy's forces being defeated and driven into the Borgo, the commissaries desired to pursue them, in order to make the victory complete, but not a single *condottiere* or soldier would obey, alleging, as a sufficient reason for their refusal, that they must take care of the booty and attend to their wounded; and, what is still more surprising, the next day, without permission from the commissaries, or the least regard for their commanders, they went to Arezzo, and, having secured their plunder, returned to Anghiari; a thing so contrary to military order and all subordination, that the merest shadow of a regular army would easily and most justly have wrested from them the victory they had so undeservedly obtained. Added to this, the men-at-arms, or heavy-armed horse, who had been taken prisoners, whom the commissaries wished to be detained that they might not rejoin the enemy, were set at liberty, contrary to their orders. It is astonishing, that an army so constructed should have sufficient energy to obtain the victory, or that any should be found so imbecile as to allow such a disorderly rabble to vanquish them."

This account, coming as it does from one of the great writers of the Italian Renaissance, has done more than any other to foster the reputation of the *condottieri* as a group of professional sham soldiers who had no interest in killing one another. It must be noted, however, that Machiavelli was against the use of mercenaries for many reasons, and he might not have been entirely objective in offering this account. Modern historian Hans Delbrück noted, "The great historians of the Renaissance, Machiavelli, Guicciardini, and Jovius, were agreed in stating that the condottieri waged war simply as a game and not in bloody earnest. It was their judgment that these men, guided by self-interest, in order to extend the war as long as possible so that they might obtain the most possible pay, did not seek a decision in battle. On the contrary, they avoided that, and when it did finally come down to a battle, the men on both sides, who regarded themselves mutually as comrades, spared one another and shed no blood. In the battle of Anghiari in 1440, for example, it is reported that one man died, to be sure, but he was not struck down but drowned in a swamp. Later scholars have no doubt characterized this kind of warfare as having raised war to a work of art, that is, the skill of maneuver, through the efforts of these *condottieri*."

Peter Paul Rubens' *The Battle of Anghiari*

While modern historians who have sifted through contemporary accounts agree that casualties among the knights were light, several hundred infantry may have been killed in the battle, but regardless of the veracity of Machiavelli's claims, there was almost unquestionably a mutual understanding between the two sides not to be too bloodthirsty. The client wanted the battle won, but if that desire could be satisfied without killing one's colleagues, all the better. Those who surrendered were generally spared and either sold for ransom or simply let go after the fighting stopped. One remarkable example of this was the aftermath of the Battle of Maclodio in 1427. The Venetian commander Carmagnola defeated the Milanese force and took about 10,000 prisoners, but he soon released them without demanding a ransom. Virtually no one was killed in this battle, although many horses were because of the stray slices of swords bouncing off the cavalrymen's thick armor and hitting the animals' necks or flanks. There are accounts of the young pages going through the field at the end of battle and dispatching the wounded, but this was a common practice in medieval and Renaissance warfare, and it may have been more mercy killing for those who wouldn't survive their wounds than a way of inflicting more casualties on the enemy.

Some battles were undoubtedly more brutal. At the Battle of Parabiago on February 20-21, 1339, the two sides suffered more than 4,000 deaths between them. It was also unusual for being fought in bitterly cold conditions in the dead of winter, a time of year when the *condottieri* preferred to stay in camp. At the Battle of Castagnaro on March 11, 1387, the Veronese had lost to the Paduans after being surrounded. Most surrendered and were treated decently, but one Veronese unit under Giovanni da Isola refused to give in and all of its men were slaughtered.

This suggests that the men's willingness to fight and die depended on circumstances, but in general, like most mercenaries, the *condottieri* did not want to risk themselves nearly as much as soldiers fighting for a cause they believed in.

As the 15th century progressed, the *condottieri* found themselves facing ever greater numbers of foreigners, consisting of either national armies or mercenaries such as the Landsknechts. These foreign troops brought different ideas of warfare with them and did not share in the Italian concepts of fair play on the battlefield. Battles became bloodier, and while the Italian mercenaries continued to win victories, they now faced a very different foe, one that in the end would defeat them.

An early battle of this type was the Battle of Motta on August 24, 1412. King Sigismund of Hungary and Croatia had just gotten through a civil war where he had emerged as sole ruler, and he found that some of what he considered his lands had been sold out from under him. He had been fighting Ladislaus of Naples, who had sold Dalmatia to the Venetian Republic for 100,000 ducats, an insultingly low figure for such a rich strip of land. Sigismund considered the sale illegal and used this as a pretext to march on Venice.

On April 20, 1411, a Hungarian army of 12,000 cavalry and 8,000 infantry crossed into Italy and enjoyed a series of successes that forced the Venetians to the negotiating table. Sigismund's demands were too great, however, and the war resumed. The *condottiero* Carlo Malatesta led 35,000 men on a major counterattack against the Hungarians that retook two castles and laid siege to the town of Motta.

By April 1412, Malatesta's force had been divided to secure the region, so he had only 12,000 men outside Motta. On April 24, the Venetian camp was suddenly attacked on three sides. The Hungarians had achieved complete surprise, but they numbered only 3,000, so they had to achieve victory quickly or the weight of being outnumbered four to one would work against them.

The Hungarians slaughtered many in the camp, and most of the Venetians who weren't killed fled in disorder, but the Hungarians, instead of consolidating their victory, resorted to looting the tents and carts. This was a common mistake among medieval and Renaissance armies, and it would prove the Hungarians' undoing. As they were scattered about searching for valuables in the tents, packs, and baggage train, Malatesta and 600 cavalry counterattacked, while one of Malatesta's commanders burnt down the bridges over a nearby river to keep the rest of the Venetians from retreating across them. Backed against the water, the rest of the Venetians rallied and helped their cavalry drive off the Hungarians, killing 1,300, including the Hungarian general, and taking 400 prisoners. The Venetians had also suffered heavily, although exact numbers are unknown. Malatesta himself was wounded, and Motta soon fell to the Venetians after an artillery bombardment.

King Sigismund personally led a new army numbering about 40,000 men on a second invasion but failed to take the city of Vicenza, losing a sizeable part of his force in the attempt. After that, he had no choice but to sue for peace.

While the Italians were victorious in the end and Venice laid claim to the western Balkans, the invasion made clear that their rivalries could be swamped by larger forces moving in. This did not stop those rivalries, but more and more often throughout the 15th century, Italian city-states found themselves having to set aside their differences for the moment in order to fight a foreign invader.

During these campaigns, the *condottieri* increasingly had to face new techniques brought in by the Swiss and the Landsknechts. The Swiss became famous in this century as pikemen, and their innovative use of closely ranked squares bristling with pikes negated much of the advantage of the *condottieri*'s heavy cavalry. The Landsknecht mercenaries from the Holy Roman Empire came a bit later and also used pike squares. Both also added handgonners and later arquebusiers into the squares to add fire support and take out the enemy from a distance.

The *condottieri*, still relying on the old style of fighting with heavy cavalry, had trouble facing these units, but they still managed to score some classic victories. One of them came at the Battle of Crevola on April 28, 1487, which came about from a dispute between the Old Swiss Confederacy and the Duchy of Milan. This was an ongoing rivalry that flared up frequently over the course of the 15th century, as the region around Milan controlled access from the Confederacy into the rest of Italy, and thus naturally both sides wanted to dominate it.

7,000 Swiss troops marched into Milan's territory and laid siege to the town of Domo as well as ravaging the nearby valleys and taking the important castle of Mattarella. The Duchy of Milan bided its time by suing for peace until it could raise a mercenary army numbering 1,200 cavalry and 2,000 infantry. While this number hardly seemed sufficient, the Swiss were predominantly infantry and thus the *condottieri* believed they were inferior troops. Furthermore, they hoped the Swiss had been lulled into a false sense of complacency because of the peace talks.

It turned out they hadn't. The Swiss soon went on a rampage through the Valle Vigezzo in the Alps, looting and burning villages as they went. Being spread out and disorganized, they did not see the Milanese force maneuvering around them until it was too late. Suddenly the Italians took the Swiss baggage train and attacked from three sides. The Swiss hurriedly formed a square with their pikes, but the savage attack, and the demoralizing awareness that they were cut off from help and retreat, destroyed the Swiss will to fight. A thousand were killed before the rest managed to escape. The Milanese, not wanting to pursue the Swiss into the Alpine passes they knew so well, let them go.

The peasants who had suffered at the hands of the invaders now took their revenge. Any wounded were dispatched in as cruel a fashion as the peasants could think of, and their heads were put on pikes. Some peasants even cut off the fingers of the dead Swiss and used them to decorate their hats.

The Old Swiss Confederacy sued for peace, but it wouldn't be long before the two sides went to war again, and a rather different result came on August 10 of the same year at the Battle of Calliano, where the Venetians were defeated by a combined force of German Landsknecht and Swiss infantry. It was unusual for these two units to be found marching side-by-side. The Swiss were already established as mercenaries, but the Landsknecht were a new force, mostly unproven in battle. They showed themselves the equals of the Swiss in pike formations and infantry tactics, and a great rivalry would subsequently ensue as the two mercenary forces vied for jobs.

The conflict started between Sigismund of Hapsburg, Duke of Austria, and the Republic of Venice over territory, as usual. A Venetian force of 1,200 cavalry and 3,000 infantry led by Italian *condottiero* Roberto Sanseverino d'Aragona (1418-1487) moved on a Tyrolean force of 200 cavalry and 1,900 infantry. On the last night of the march, the two armies found themselves camped on opposite sides of the Adige River with no bridge nearby. The Tyroleans assumed they were safe, but Roberto Sanseverino had his engineers swim across the river, secure lines, and build a floating bridge. He then moved his force across the river to besiege two small forts protecting the area and provoke a response from the Tyrolean force by looting the area they had claimed as their own.

They got the response they wanted, with the Tyroleans attacking the smaller Venetian infantry detachments besieging one of the forts who fled toward the floating bridge for safety. The Venetian cavalry held the position against the pursuing Tyroleans and a bitter two-hour fight ensued. Then some Tyrolean reinforcements showed up and attacked the Venetians on both flanks.

This was the last straw. With most of the infantry broken and standing around doing nothing by the riverside, the Venetian cavalry tried to flee across the bridge, pushing their own infantry before them. The bridge soon became overloaded and collapsed, plunging hundreds of heavily armored men into the water to drown. Roberto Sanseverino d'Aragona was among those who ended up sinking to the bottom.

Another major defeat came at the Battle of Agnadello on April 15, 1509. King Louis XII of France had secured Milan and decided to move on Venice as his next conquest. He led an army of 30,000 men, but facing him was Italian *condottieri* captains Bartolomeo d'Alviano (1455-1515) and his cousin Niccolò di Pitigliano (1442–1510) at the head of a force 15,000 strong. They had been given orders to avoid battle with the larger French force and thus spent their time skirmishing with the invaders, trying to slow their advance and keep them from sending out units to pillage the countryside. This was a common tactic that could often wear down an invading army, but the French would not be stopped, so both armies continued moving south. Pitigliano was in the vanguard, with Bartolomeo d'Alviano a little behind and the French not far behind him. When Bartolomeo got word that his rearguard had been overtaken and attacked by a large French vanguard, he turned around to give assistance. He had 8,000 men with him and positioned them on a ridge cut with irrigation ditches overlooking some vineyards. It was a strong position, but nevertheless the French felt that with their superior numbers, they could overwhelm the Venetians.

The French cavalry rode up to smash the defenders, but the French quickly got bogged down in the muddy irrigation ditches filled by heavy rainfall and had to withdraw. The cavalry in those days relied on their momentum to break the line, and if that momentum was itself broken, they were much less effective.

Next, the French sent up their Swiss mercenary pikemen, but once again the attack got bogged down due to the muddy slope and withering fire from the Venetian arquebusiers and artillery. They, too, had to withdraw.

Despite staving off two assaults, Bartolomeo d'Alviano had grown worried. He was greatly outnumbered and sent word to his cousin to come help. The reply he received was a curt note saying they had been ordered not to engage in battle. Pitigliano thus continued to move south with nearly half the available Venetian force.

By this time, the rest of the French force had arrived. They doubly enveloped the Venetian army and began to squeeze. The Venetians fought valiantly for three hours, but the weight of numbers began to tell. In a final desperate bid, Bartolomeo led his heavy cavalry right at the French center. The French line buckled, but did not break, and soon the Venetian cavalry was hemmed in, fighting on all sides. Bartolomeo fell wounded and ended up a prisoner. Seeing their leader fall, the rest of the Venetian army fled, leaving behind 4,000 dead, many captured, and losing most if not all of their artillery.

When word of the utter defeat reached Pitigliano's force, most of his men deserted. Venice had to sue for a humiliating peace, and as Machiavelli wrote in *The Prince*, the city-state "lost what it had taken them eight hundred years' exertion to conquer."

The End of an Era

The *condottieri* were to a large degree victims of their own tactics. Once considered innovative for their knowledge of Roman military manuals and their forceful use of disciplined armored cavalry, they relied on their increasingly outdated cavalry tactics long after the era of the knight had passed. By the late 15th century, the balance of power on the battlefield was steadily turning in favor of the infantry as crude handgonnes were giving way to more accurate and powerful muskets, and pike formations still made walls of sharp points that proved difficult for cavalry to break through. While the *condottieri* did use infantry, they never used them to their full potential like some of their more innovative contemporaries. The *condottieri* had had it too easy for too long, ruling the roost and showing off in their fine armor and warhorses, while the technology and tactics of military science in other parts of Europe outpaced them.

Some Italian city-states responded by hiring the more successful Swiss and Landsknecht units, but this was not a practice for terribly long because other factors led to a decline in the use of mercenaries in Italy. In essence, even if the *condottieri* had updated their tactics, their days would have still been numbered. Political and economic factors were changing the landscape, and while Italy would not unify as a nation until the 19th century, there was a gradual consolidation of territory, with smaller states being absorbed into larger ones. These states were better able to raise their own armies to face the greater challenges of staving off invasions from the armies of Spain, France, and the Holy Roman Empire. By 1550, the practice of the *condotta* had disappeared, and a new era of warfare was at hand.

While the *condottieri* faded out quickly in the 16th century, the *condottieri* had left a lasting mark on Italian politics. They established many noble houses and grand traditions, becoming both the patrons and the subjects of some of the Renaissance's greatest artists. The Sforza family, for example, were dukes of Milan for six generations and were patrons in that city-state for much of the Italian Renaissance. Other members of the Sforza family held many important political positions or went into the Church and rose to prominent positions in the Papal States.

The Sforzas were not alone. Many other *condottieri* became important leaders in the city-states they had been hired to protect. Bartolomeo Colleoni, for example, was a major player in the politics of Venice in the 15th century, as was Erasmo da Narni. Both have been immortalized in impressive statues that can still be seen in the beautiful city to this day, permanent proof that as brutal and double-dealing as the *condottieri* could be, they are an indelible part of Italy's history.

A portrait of Colleoni

Didier Descousins' picture of the equestrian statue of Colleoni in Venice

Donatello's statue of Erasmo da Narni in Venice

Online Resources

Other medieval history titles by Charles River Editors & Sean McLachlan

Other titles about *condottieri* on Amazon

Bibliography

Appelbaum, Stanley. *The Triumph of Maximilian I.* Mineola, New York City, New York: Dover Publications, Inc., 1964.

Bennet, Matthew, et al. *Fighting Techniques of the Medieval World AD 500-AD 1500: Equipment, Combat Skills and Tactics.* Staplehurst, Kent, United Kingdom: Spellmount Ltd, 2005.

Bennett, Matthew and Christer Jorgensen, Michael Pavkovic, Rob S. Rice, Frederick S. Schneid, Chris Scott. *Fighting Techniques of the Early Modern World 1500-1763.* London, United Kingdom: Amber Books Ltd., 2005.

Browning, Oscar. *The Age of the Condottieri.* London, United Kingdom: Methuen & Co., 1895.

Burkhardt, Jacob. *The Civilization of the Renaissance.* New York City, New York: Penguin Books, 1990.

Charles River Editors and Sean McLachlan. *Warfare in the Middle Ages: The History of Medieval Military and Siege Tactics.* Charles River Editors: 2015.

Charles River Editors and Sean McLachlan. *Warfare in the Era of Pike and Shot: The History and Legacy of the Military Strategies that Ushered in Modern Warfare.* Charles River Editors: 2017.

Charles River Editors and Sean McLachlan. *The Landsknechts: The History and Legacy of the German Mercenaries Who Fought for the Holy Roman Empire.* Charles River Editors: 2020.

Davies, Jonathan. *The Medieval Cannon 1326-1494.* Oxford, United Kingdom: Osprey Publishing, 2019.

DeVries, Kelly. *Medieval Military Technology.* Peterborough, Ontario, Canada: Broadview Press Ltd, 1992.

Hale, J. R. *War and Society in Renaissance Europe 1450–1620.* Stroud, United Kingdom: Sutton Publishing, 1998.

Hall, Bert. *Weapons and Warfare in Renaissance Europe.* London, United Kingdom: The John Hopkins University Press, 2001.

Hogg, O. F. G. *Artillery: Its Origin, Heyday, and Decline.* London, United Kingdom: C. Hurst & Co, 1970.

Machiavelli, Niccolo. *The Florentine History*. London, United Kingdom: Archibald Constable & Co. Ltd., 1906.

McLachlan, Sean. *Medieval Handgonnes: The First Black Powder Infantry Weapons*. Oxford, United Kingdom: Osprey Publishing, 2010.

Mallett, Michael. *Mercenaries and their Masters: Warfare in Renaissance Italy*. London, United Kingdom: The Bodley Head, 1974.

Miller, Artur Maximilian. *The Landsknechts*. Oxford, United Kingdom: Osprey Publishing, 1976

Miller, Douglas, and Embleton, Gerry. *The Swiss at War 1300–1500*. Oxford, United Kingdom: Osprey Publishing, 1998.

Murphy, David. *Condottiere 1300-1500: Infamous Medieval Mercenaries*. Oxford, United Kingdom: Osprey Publishing, 2007.

Nicolle, David. *Italian Medieval Armies 1300–1500*. Oxford, United Kingdom: Osprey Publishing, 1983.

Nicolle, David. *Medieval Warfare Source Book, vols I & II*. London, United Kingdom: Arms and Armour Press, 1995.

Richards, John. *Landsknecht Soldier 1486-1560*. Oxford, United Kingdom: Osprey Publishing, 2002.

Roberts, Keith. *Pike and Shot Tactics 1590-1660*. Oxford, United Kingdom: Osprey Publishing, 2010.

Free Books by Charles River Editors

We have brand new titles available for free most days of the week. To see which of our titles are currently free, click on this link.

Discounted Books by Charles River Editors

We have titles at a discount price of just 99 cents everyday. To see which of our titles are currently 99 cents, click on this link.